with

Candace Kentridge-Britton

BEGINNERS GUIDE TO
SUSTAINABLE
LIVING

Introduction:

As most of us know there has never been a more important time on our planet for humans to live a sustainable lifestyle. This is not only necessary for the existence, continuance and well-being of the planet but it can be an amazing way for families to save money and learn to run their homes in a more natural way free of chemicals and toxins. You could read articles, blog posts and watch documentaries on various aspects such as climate change, the massive impact that plastic has on our oceans, the billions of tons of waste that is accumulated and wonder "where do I even begin" or perhaps you have started implementing small changes into your lifestyle already that will allow for a more sustainable lifestyle and therefore reduce your carbon footprint.

The 6 steps that I am going to talk about are a great starting point and will allow anyone to start creating new habits, become more aware and be able to share this knowledge with others. Have you ever looked at how much plastic we as humans consume on a daily basis (very often unaware of it)?

I was an advocate for recycling for many years and then in 2018 I watched a documentary on plastic waste and my views completely changed. I learned that only 9% of all waste set to be recycled will actually successfully be recycled. I realized that I absolutely had to do more than just taking my plastic, glass and paper to a recycle depot. I felt overwhelmed and didn't really know how I was going to achieve this or make a difference so I began with YouTube videos on sustainable living and I was so impressed to find out how many other people felt the same way as I did; people of all ages and from so many different countries. I decided to start with a few steps; creating new habits in my lifestyle I would then be able to slowly keep improving and doing more and more. I try and encourage friends and family to adopt the same steps, I always try to create awareness wherever I can and I love the feeling that my actions will have a positive effect on the planet. You may not feel that one person can make a difference but it starts with one person and when each individual starts making changes the difference goes from 1 to limitless.

BAG
FOR
LIFE

TAKE YOUR OWN REUSABLE SHOPPING BAGS WHEN YOU GO GROCERY SHOPPING:

Disposable shopping bags are convenient, but they are a major source of waste and pollution on our planet. Plastic shopping bags on land are one of the most common types of litter. Plastic bags are well known to block local drainage systems, especially in developing countries. For example, the floods in Bangladesh 20 years ago were partially attributed to blockages in drainage systems from plastic shopping bags.

Plastic shopping bags also pose health risks to human populations over the years as they leach toxins into water supplies. Plastic bags are also difficult to recycle. While the recyclable symbol of the three arrows in a circle is on many plastic shopping bags in the US, there are no regulations about how that symbol is used, and every city and county in America has different regulations about what can be recycled.

Many plastic bags that are collected by recycling companies **cannot really be recycled**. Most of these bags actually **end up in landfills and sit there for hundreds of years**. Floating plastic shopping bags can be mistaken to be jellyfish by marine animals who consume them. One of the many species that are at risk from the bags is sea turtles. They risk extinction because of ingesting large amounts of plastics. The plastic festers in their stomach because the plastic cannot be digested. Plastic bags are not just on land, plastic shopping bags have heavily contributed to huge amounts of plastic found in the North Pacific Ocean. **Wild Studies Institute** has reported that as all drains go to the ocean, 80% of the trash in the ocean originated from land. **The use of reusable shopping bags will have a HUGE positive impact on the planet and once you create this habit it is really an easy one to keep doing.**

START BULK SHOPPING TO AVOID PLASTIC PACKAGING:

If you were to examine your trash, you will likely see that food packaging makes up a large proportion of what you throw out. Packaging waste takes up a huge amount of space in our kitchen bins and, ultimately, in landfills. It is often made from plastic, which is wasteful to produce, and even though it is technically recyclable, can often only be down cycled. There are studies that say plastic packaging may be harmful to health, due to the chemicals they can contain.

Buying in bulk is a fantastic way to use less plastic and reduce packaging waste, cut down what we accumulate and throw away in the kitchen. Making the switch can seem daunting at first but like anything with a little practice it will become part of your daily / weekly and monthly shopping habits. Modern packaging is designed for convenience, and most of us have formed habits around using it. You can become a more "planet-friendly shopper" by taking your own containers and produce bags to a bulk store. At bulk stores and some regular grocery stores, you can pay for your goods by weight by first removing the weight of your containers from the price. This process is known as tarring. Zero waste stores with an Eco-conscious supply chain are one of the least wasteful ways to shop. There are more bulk stores around now than ever so be sure to have a look for one in your area. Bring appropriate containers for the food you want to buy (a shopping list will help). Jars are great for bulk items while bread, fruit and vegetables can be put into cloth bags. You can also use mesh bags which you don't need to tare because they are just as light as standard plastic ones. Shopping at a farmer's market, if you have one nearby, often allows you to buy exactly what you need while reducing packaging waste and your carbon footprint. The food there is often local and unpackaged. You may also feel more connected to the producers of the food you are buying, meaning there is more incentive not to waste it.

This checklist is a great way to make sure of what to bring with you when you shop:

- Reusable shopping bags

- Cloth bags / Produce bags for fresh food

- Jars or glass containers for bulk items

SWITCH TO BATHROOM & KITCHEN PRODUCTS WITH SUSTAINABLE PACKAGING:

When we stop and really access the products we have in our bathroom and kitchen, it may come as a shock to see the amount of plastic we are actually consuming. A bamboo toothbrush is the first swap I always suggest, and then I would suggest swapping disposable razors for a metal or a non-plastic razor, using a shampoo soap bar (and conditioner soap bar) packaged in a tin or Eco-friendly container instead of plastic bottles, switching from cotton wool pads to reusable Eco-friendly cleansing pads and tampons to menstrual cups, and either seeking out an Eco-friendly packaged mouthwash and toothpaste or what I simply do is make my own (toothpaste & mouth wash). It is not a secret that disposable razors are wasteful, they are designed to be used a few times and then thrown in the garbage, they are also not easily recyclable. And if we continue buying them, companies will continue making them. Since most of them are made of plastic, that means continued use of fossil fuels for a product that will probably end up in a landfill. Disposable razors are usually made of several different materials, which make them a challenge to recycle properly: There is the handle, which often contains both plastic and some sort of rubber for grip, and the head or cartridge, which includes the metal blades embedded in a plastic frame. Plastic toothbrushes pollute the environment and end up in our oceans and washed up on our beaches or consumed by marine life, harming them and potentially killing them.

Most of this plastic gets broken down into smaller pieces, these small pieces end up being ingested by nearby marine life. **Over a billion toothbrushes end up in landfills every year in North America, this is just in North America; now imagine all other countries also contribute to that!** On average, **300 million tons of plastic are produced around the globe each year.** Considering dentists recommend that you replace your toothbrush once every two months, most people go through a couple toothbrushes per year.

That may not seem like a very large impact at first glance, but consider how many people live on this planet and if everyone is throwing out a few brushes a year it adds up very quickly. Electric toothbrushes leak toxins into the environment, electric toothbrushes are also typically made of plastic and rubber and have the added negativity of requiring batteries that when not disposed of properly causing terrible damage to the environment.

Even rechargeable batteries end up needing to be replaced over time and these batteries often get discarded into landfills where the battery acid leaks into nearby oceans and waterways harming wildlife and the environment. Plastic toothbrushes are made from a combination of plastic material derived from crude oil, rubber and a mix of plastic and cardboard for the packaging so, it is not just the disposal of the brushes that are the issue. The manufacturing process for plastic toothbrushes contains harmful plastic by-products as well as petroleum and crude oil. **Plastic toothbrushes take over 400 years to decompose, they remain in landfills indefinitely.** As they settle into the landfill, they release chemicals into the air, resulting in even more damage to the environment. **Toothbrushes made from bamboo are a** renewable alternative that have the added benefit of being **100% biodegradable**. Bamboo toothbrushes are also antimicrobial; this means that your toothbrush won't be at risk for growing all kinds of nasty bacteria. If you want to move into a greener future, buy a bamboo toothbrush. Try a dish washing soap bar instead of buying dish washing liquid in a plastic bottle; you can store the soap on a wood or tin soap holder and style this in your kitchen. Another easy swap in the kitchen is laundry liquid; try an Eco-friendly packaged laundry detergent, just by doing some research online this will be an easy and awesome swap to make. Very often the Eco-friendly products are also much better for your skin and clothing. Like anything new, it takes some time to adjust to change but these "swaps" will not only simplify your life and save you money but you will be contributing to saving the planet in a very big way. Gradual change can be especially helpful for those on a tight budget, If you make a list of all the plastic items you have in your bathroom and kitchen and then list the alternatives you want to swap them for, you can then budget to make a couple of swaps each month. Some of the fantastic online options I have found are **thegreenerplace.com** and Natural Vegan **habitatbotanicals.com**

There are also great options on Facebook to join groups that promote sustainable and Eco-friendly living. This is a great way to try and connect with others potentially in your area, also making these changes.

THRIFT SHOPPING:

I personally love thrift shopping and have very often found amazing items at such reasonable prices and I know when I support thrift shopping I am reducing the amount of clothing waste that is dumped in landfills. Why thrift you might think? Well, when you thrift shop you are re-wearing clothes and therefore reducing waste and pollution, second-hand clothes are less likely to end up in landfills, Thrift stores make it easier to know where your money is going, many thrift stores directly support charities, thrifting is cheaper and secondhand clothing is often of a higher quality than comparatively-priced clothing. In addition to the positive environmental factors that Thrift shopping has, Thrifted clothing offers more room for uniqueness allowing you to pick up bargains (literally very often jeans and dresses for $1) and not go out to find 10 or more

other people wearing the same item as you; which may happen when you shop at popular franchise stores. I wasn't very open minded to Thrift shopping in the beginning however over the past 3 years since moving into a more sustainable lifestyle, I have actually come to LOVE Thrift shopping. It can feel like a treasure hunt and I have found some amazing items at really ridiculously low prices. For me personally a big part of sustainable living naturally comes, minimalism and on my personal journey minimalism actually came first. Once I started cleaning out my wardrobe regularly I would ask myself:

1 **What do I use**

2 **What do I love**

3 **What do I need**

I became so aware of waste, mindless shopping and just accumulating so much which was unnecessary and often not really used. Have you ever heard the expression "a closet full of clothes and nothing to wear"? It is amazing how much more I enjoy choosing outfits now and my wardrobe is less than half of what it was a few years ago. If I know I really need something I will never "impulse buy" but rather keep trying thrift stores and wait until I find exactly what I am looking for. I also make sure to keep (each new season) going through my wardrobe and cleaning it out. I will ask myself "if I was shopping now would I buy this?" and if the answer is "no" then I happily donate it to a thrift store or charity so that someone else can enjoy it. Simply switching to Thrifting isn't going to completely solve all of the problems within the fashion and textile industry, however it is one way we can work to minimize our own carbon footprint and make small steps towards a better greener future. Go with some friends and have fun exploring the Thrift stores in your area.

17

YOGA & HEALTH WITH
CANDACE

BUY A GLASS OR PREFERRED REUSABLE WATER BOTTLE:

Switching to a reusable water bottle will decrease the oil used, greenhouse gasses emitted, and bottles thrown away, reducing the pollution threefold. Aside from environmental benefits, reusable water bottles have many other advantages over disposable ones. Plastic bottles are made from PET (Polyethylene Terephthalate). Many of the chemicals that go into the production of plastic bottles continue to leach out into the air and into the water they hold. Research warns us that chemicals in plastic can seep into our food and lead to major health effects like obesity, heart disease, and diabetes. Chemicals in plastic called BPA and phthalates seem to be everywhere. Many researchers worry these chemicals can leach into food and get into your body. Today, the convenience of disposable water bottles means that we can find bottled water almost everywhere we go. There is no doubt that plastic bottles (and bottled water) are bad for the environment, not only do they require a lot of energy to manufacture, but they pollute the environment as well.

Plastic cannot be recycled by living organisms. Instead, a combination of the sun's energy and environmental factors like rain will continue to degrade plastic down into smaller and smaller pieces. These pieces of plastic (also known as **micro plastics) will always remain on Earth as plastic.** It can take up to **1000 years for a plastic bottle to degrade.** However, **plastic bottles do not biodegrade,** so they will remain in our environment forever. When plastic degrades, toxic chemicals in the plastic are released into the environment. Worse yet, any plastic that makes it into the environment will stay in the environment, forever harming wildlife in the future. One big problem with plastic, of course, is that its production requires the use of non-renewable fossil fuels, the energy used for transportation, storage, and the final disposal of the bottle. When you switch to a reusable water bottle not only will you be helping to save the environment, but you will also save money in the long run.

RIDE YOUR BICYCLE
WHENEVER YOU CAN:

Bike riding uses minimal fossil fuels and is a pollution-free mode of transport. Bikes reduce the need to build, service and dispose of cars. Cycling 10 km each way to work would save 1500 kg of greenhouse gas emissions each year. Riding your bicycle, or cycling, has countless benefits. These can range from personal, to economic, to social, to environmental and more. Cycling is a good form of exercise. It is also a simple, Eco-friendly transportation option. Due to cycling's many benefits, more people in the world own bicycles than cars. The more cars we can get off the road, the better it will be for the environment.

Cycling requires no gasoline and, therefore, no harmful vehicle emissions or smog are released into the air when a person is riding his or her bicycle. Opting to use your bicycle a few times a week, instead of your car, is one of the simplest ways to lower your carbon footprint. Cycling is a simple way to get around town, commute and explore new places. Even if you can't ride your bike all the way to work, many buses and trains have places where cyclists can store their bikes in between stops. This way you can ride your bike, and use public transportation when needed, to commute. Cycling is a fun way you can reduce your carbon footprint and there are many health benefits as well.

Remember to start with small changes and as these small habits become easier and easier, you will be able to keep adding more "swaps" and Eco-friendly alternatives to your home and habits; aiming towards living a more sustainable lifestyle. It feels good to know that on a daily basis you are trying to be part of the solution and care for our beautiful planet and all its creatures. Humans have the power to affect change and it is up to each individual to start making those changes. A little can go a long way.

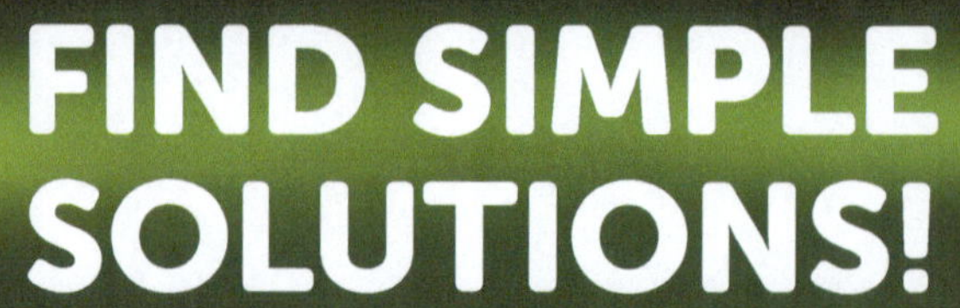

FIND SIMPLE
SOLUTIONS!

Candace
Kentridge-Britton

Special thanks to:

Brandi Brown
Tahoe Production House

www.yogahealthcandace.com